EMMANUEL JOSEPH

Innovators vs. Investors, A Human Comparison of Silicon Valley and Real Estate Billionaires

Copyright © 2025 by Emmanuel Joseph

All rights reserved. No part of this publication may be reproduced, stored or transmitted in any form or by any means, electronic, mechanical, photocopying, recording, scanning, or otherwise without written permission from the publisher. It is illegal to copy this book, post it to a website, or distribute it by any other means without permission.

First edition

This book was professionally typeset on Reedsy.
Find out more at reedsy.com

Contents

1 Chapter 1   1
2 Chapter 1: The Dawn of Two Empires   3
3 Chapter 2: The Mindsets that Shape Empires   5
4 Chapter 3: The Role of Education and Experience   7
5 Chapter 5: The Impact on Society   10
6 Chapter 6: Navigating Economic Challenges   12
7 Chapter 7: Philanthropy and Social Responsibility   14
8 Chapter 8: The Influence of Technology   16
9 Chapter 9: The Power of Networks   18
10 Chapter 10: Navigating Regulation and Policy   20
11 Chapter 11: The Future of Wealth   22
12 Chapter 12: Lessons from the Titans   24

1

Chapter 1

Introduction

In a world where wealth and success are often admired and scrutinized, the paths taken by the elite to reach the pinnacle of financial prosperity are as varied as the individuals themselves. "Innovators vs. Investors: A Human Comparison of Silicon Valley and Real Estate Billionaires" delves into the contrasting journeys of two distinct groups who have shaped our modern economy in profound ways. Silicon Valley innovators, with their relentless drive for technological advancement, and real estate investors, with their strategic acquisition of tangible assets, represent two sides of the same coin. This book seeks to explore the unique characteristics, strategies, and impacts of these billionaires, providing a comprehensive comparison that highlights their contributions to society.

The world of Silicon Valley is a hotbed of innovation, where disruptive ideas are transformed into groundbreaking technologies that redefine industries. Innovators in this realm are characterized by their willingness to take risks, their relentless pursuit of progress, and their ability to pivot in the face of failure. Companies like Apple, Google, and Tesla have not only revolutionized their respective fields but have also created new markets and opportunities. The stories of these tech giants are a testament to the power of creativity and the belief that technology can change the world for the better.

On the other hand, real estate investors operate in a domain that is grounded in tangible assets and long-term stability. Their wealth is built on the foundation of strategic acquisitions, development projects, and the ability to foresee market trends. Real estate moguls have the unique ability to shape the physical landscape of our cities, creating spaces that foster economic growth and community development. From commercial skyscrapers to residential complexes, their investments have a lasting impact on the fabric of society. Their approach is often marked by pragmatism, patience, and a keen understanding of market dynamics.

While both Silicon Valley innovators and real estate investors have achieved tremendous success, their paths are marked by distinct differences in mindset, strategy, and impact. Innovators thrive on disruption and the constant evolution of technology, while investors seek stability and incremental growth through tangible assets. This book explores these contrasting approaches, delving into the psychological frameworks, educational backgrounds, and experiences that shape these leaders. By understanding their unique journeys, we gain insights into the diverse ways wealth can be created and sustained.

"**Innovators vs. Investors**" is more than just a comparison of two groups of billionaires; it is a study of the human spirit and the various ways it manifests in the pursuit of success. Through detailed case studies, thought-provoking analysis, and compelling narratives, this book offers a comprehensive and humanized perspective on the dynamics of wealth-building. Whether you're an aspiring entrepreneur, an investor, or simply curious about the forces shaping our economy, this book provides valuable lessons and inspiration for anyone seeking to understand the intricate world of innovation and investment.

2

Chapter 1: The Dawn of Two Empires

The world of wealth is often categorized into two distinct realms: the innovators of Silicon Valley and the investors in real estate. Both have crafted empires, but their journeys are markedly different. Innovators, with their penchant for disruption, embrace the unknown, leveraging technology to create unprecedented solutions. On the other hand, real estate investors rely on tangible assets, transforming landscapes and economies through strategic acquisitions and developments. By understanding their beginnings, we can better appreciate the unique paths they've carved.

The origins of Silicon Valley are steeped in a culture of innovation and risk-taking. The region's transformation into a tech powerhouse was fueled by a confluence of factors, including a strong academic presence, venture capital, and a spirit of entrepreneurship. Early pioneers, such as Hewlett-Packard and Intel, laid the groundwork for what would become a global hub for technology and innovation.

Conversely, the world of real estate investment has a longer history rooted in the development of cities and infrastructure. Real estate moguls have shaped the physical landscape, building skyscrapers, residential complexes, and commercial spaces that drive economic growth. Their wealth is tied to tangible assets, making their journey less volatile but equally impactful.

This chapter delves into the rise of tech giants and real estate moguls, tracing the factors that contributed to their success. Through historical context and key examples, we explore how these two worlds emerged and evolved over time.

By understanding the origins of these two realms, we gain insight into the motivations and strategies that drive their respective billionaires. The chapter sets the stage for a deeper exploration of the unique paths and mindsets that define Silicon Valley innovators and real estate investors.

3

Chapter 2: The Mindsets that Shape Empires

At the heart of every empire lies a distinct mindset. Innovators are driven by a relentless pursuit of progress and a belief in the transformative power of technology. They thrive on risks, often viewing failures as stepping stones to success. Contrastingly, real estate investors are grounded in pragmatism and long-term vision. They seek stability and incremental growth, valuing tangible assets over abstract concepts.

The mindset of a tech innovator is characterized by a willingness to embrace uncertainty and a desire to change the world. These individuals often possess a deep passion for their work and a vision for the future that drives them to push boundaries. Their ability to pivot and adapt to new challenges is a testament to their resilience and creativity.

On the other hand, real estate investors approach their endeavors with a focus on stability and strategic planning. They prioritize thorough research and due diligence, ensuring that their investments yield steady returns. Their success is built on a foundation of calculated risks and a keen understanding of market dynamics.

This chapter explores the psychological frameworks that propel these billionaires, offering insights into their decision-making processes and what fuels their ambitions. By comparing and contrasting the mindsets of Silicon Valley innovators and real estate investors, we gain a deeper appreciation for the diverse approaches to building wealth and empires.

Understanding the mindsets that shape these empires allows us to appreciate the unique strengths and challenges faced by tech innovators and real estate moguls. It also provides valuable lessons for aspiring entrepreneurs and investors seeking to emulate their success.

4

Chapter 3: The Role of Education and Experience

The paths to billionaire status are as diverse as the individuals who tread them. Many tech innovators boast prestigious educational backgrounds, with a heavy emphasis on engineering and computer science. Their experiences often include stints in cutting-edge startups or leading tech firms, where they hone their skills and build crucial networks. Conversely, real estate moguls might not always come from elite universities but instead possess a deep understanding of market dynamics and a knack for spotting lucrative opportunities.

Education plays a significant role in shaping the careers of Silicon Valley innovators. Institutions like Stanford and MIT have produced numerous tech leaders, providing them with the knowledge and resources needed to excel in the industry. These innovators often participate in tech incubators and accelerators, gaining valuable insights and mentorship that propel their careers forward.

Real estate investors, on the other hand, often learn through hands-on experience and mentorship from industry veterans. They develop a keen eye for market trends and opportunities, leveraging their expertise to make strategic investments. While formal education is important, the real-world experience and intuition gained through years of practice are equally crucial in their success.

This chapter examines the educational and experiential journeys that shape these leaders, highlighting the critical moments that define their careers. By exploring the diverse paths taken by tech innovators and real estate moguls, we gain a better understanding of the factors that contribute to their success.

The role of education and experience in shaping these billionaires offers valuable insights for aspiring entrepreneurs and investors. It underscores the importance of continuous learning, adaptability, and the willingness to seize opportunities as they arise.

Chapter 4: Innovations vs. Investments: Risk and Reward

In the high-stakes game of wealth-building, the approach to risk and reward can be a defining factor. Innovators are often seen as gamblers, betting on untested technologies and uncharted markets. Their rewards can be astronomical, but the risks are equally daunting. Real estate investors, however, play a different game. They invest in stability, with calculated risks that promise steady returns.

The risk profile of a tech innovator is characterized by a willingness to embrace failure as part of the journey. They understand that not every venture will succeed, but the ones that do can revolutionize industries and generate immense wealth. This mindset allows them to take bold steps and explore uncharted territories, often leading to groundbreaking discoveries and innovations.

Real estate investors, in contrast, prioritize risk mitigation and steady growth. They focus on acquiring properties that offer reliable income streams and appreciate in value over time. Their investments are backed by thorough research and a deep understanding of market dynamics, ensuring that their portfolios remain resilient in the face of economic fluctuations.

This chapter contrasts the risk profiles of these two groups, shedding light on their strategies for managing uncertainty and maximizing gains. Through detailed case studies, we explore the successes and failures that have defined their legacies.

By comparing the approaches to risk and reward in Silicon Valley and real estate, we gain a deeper appreciation for the diverse strategies employed by

CHAPTER 3: THE ROLE OF EDUCATION AND EXPERIENCE

these billionaires. It also offers valuable lessons for those looking to navigate the complex landscape of wealth-building.

5

Chapter 5: The Impact on Society

Both Silicon Valley innovators and real estate investors have left indelible marks on society, though in different ways. Tech billionaires have revolutionized how we communicate, work, and live, ushering in an era of unprecedented connectivity and convenience. Their innovations have not only driven economic growth but also sparked debates on privacy, ethics, and the future of work. In contrast, real estate moguls have shaped the physical landscape, developing infrastructure, housing, and commercial spaces that foster community growth and economic stability.

The impact of tech innovators is evident in the rapid advancement of digital technologies and their integration into everyday life. From smartphones and social media to artificial intelligence and autonomous vehicles, their creations have transformed industries and reshaped how we interact with the world. However, these advancements also raise important questions about data privacy, job displacement, and the ethical implications of emerging technologies.

Real estate investors, on the other hand, have a more tangible impact on society. Their developments create jobs, stimulate local economies, and provide essential infrastructure. By investing in commercial properties, residential complexes, and urban renewal projects, they contribute to the growth and stability of communities. However, their actions can also lead to gentrification and displacement, raising important social and ethical considerations.

This chapter delves into the societal impacts of these two groups, exploring their contributions and controversies. By examining the broader implications of their actions, we gain a deeper understanding of the role they play in shaping our world.

Understanding the impact of Silicon Valley innovators and real estate investors on society offers valuable insights into the responsibilities and challenges faced by these billionaires. It also highlights the importance of balancing economic growth with social and ethical considerations.

6

Chapter 6: Navigating Economic Challenges

Economic downturns and market volatility pose significant challenges for both tech innovators and real estate investors. How they navigate these challenges reveals much about their resilience and strategic thinking. Innovators may pivot quickly, leveraging new technologies or business models to weather the storm. Real estate investors, meanwhile, might focus on diversifying their portfolios or investing in recession-proof assets.

During economic downturns, tech innovators often turn to innovation and adaptability as key strategies for survival. They may pivot their business models, explore new markets, or develop cost-saving technologies to maintain profitability. Their ability to quickly respond to changing conditions and identify new opportunities is a testament to their resilience and creativity.

Real estate investors, on the other hand, prioritize diversification and risk management. They may shift their focus to recession-proof assets such as affordable housing, healthcare facilities, or essential retail spaces. By maintaining a balanced and diversified portfolio, they can mitigate the impact of economic fluctuations and ensure steady returns.

This chapter examines how these billionaires adapt to economic shifts, drawing lessons from their ability to thrive in uncertain times. Through case studies and examples, we explore the strategies employed by tech innovators and real estate investors to navigate economic challenges.

By understanding how Silicon Valley innovators and real estate moguls navigate economic challenges, we gain valuable insights into their resilience and strategic thinking. It also offers lessons for those looking to build and sustain wealth in an ever-changing economic landscape.

7

Chapter 7: Philanthropy and Social Responsibility

With great wealth comes great responsibility. Both Silicon Valley and real estate billionaires have embraced philanthropy, using their fortunes to address societal issues. Tech leaders often channel their resources into education, healthcare, and environmental causes, leveraging their expertise to drive change. Real estate moguls, on the other hand, might focus on community development, affordable housing, and urban renewal.

Tech innovators like Bill Gates and Elon Musk have set an example by funding initiatives aimed at eradicating diseases, advancing renewable energy, and improving global education. Their contributions often go beyond financial support, as they bring their problem-solving skills and networks to bear on these issues. By tackling some of the world's most pressing challenges, they strive to make a lasting impact.

Real estate investors, such as Donald Bren and Stephen Ross, focus on creating sustainable and inclusive communities. They invest in affordable housing projects, infrastructure development, and public spaces that enhance the quality of life for residents. Their philanthropic efforts aim to address housing shortages, promote economic growth, and foster social cohesion.

This chapter explores the philanthropic endeavors of these billionaires,

CHAPTER 7: PHILANTHROPY AND SOCIAL RESPONSIBILITY

highlighting their contributions and the motivations behind their giving. By examining their approaches to philanthropy, we gain insight into their values and the legacy they aim to leave behind.

Understanding the philanthropic efforts of Silicon Valley and real estate billionaires offers valuable lessons for those looking to make a positive impact. It underscores the importance of using wealth and influence to address societal issues and improve the lives of others.

8

Chapter 8: The Influence of Technology

For tech innovators, technology is both the means and the end. They continuously push the boundaries of what's possible, driving progress across industries. Real estate investors, too, are increasingly embracing technology, using it to enhance efficiency, sustainability, and profitability. From smart buildings to AI-driven market analysis, technology is reshaping the real estate landscape.

Innovators like Jeff Bezos and Mark Zuckerberg have leveraged technology to revolutionize commerce, communication, and entertainment. Their companies, Amazon and Facebook, have transformed how we shop, connect, and consume information. These technological advancements have created new business models and opportunities, driving economic growth and changing societal norms.

Real estate investors are also harnessing the power of technology to improve their operations and offerings. Smart buildings equipped with IoT devices enhance energy efficiency, security, and occupant comfort. AI-driven market analysis helps investors make data-informed decisions, optimizing their portfolios for maximum returns. This integration of technology into real estate is creating smarter, more sustainable cities.

This chapter examines the role of technology in both worlds, exploring how it influences strategies and outcomes. By comparing the technological advancements in Silicon Valley and real estate, we gain a deeper understanding of the innovative approaches that drive their success.

The influence of technology on both Silicon Valley innovators and real estate investors underscores the importance of embracing innovation and leveraging data to stay ahead in a competitive landscape.

9

Chapter 9: The Power of Networks

In the world of billionaires, relationships are paramount. Innovators often benefit from tight-knit networks of investors, advisors, and fellow entrepreneurs. These connections can provide crucial support, resources, and opportunities. Real estate investors also rely heavily on networks, building relationships with financiers, developers, and political figures.

Silicon Valley's success is often attributed to its vibrant ecosystem of venture capitalists, tech incubators, and industry events. Innovators like Larry Page and Sergey Brin of Google benefited from the guidance and support of experienced mentors and investors. These networks facilitate knowledge-sharing, collaboration, and access to capital, driving the growth of tech startups.

Real estate investors, such as Sam Zell and Richard LeFrak, cultivate relationships with key stakeholders in the industry. They collaborate with developers, architects, and city planners to bring their projects to life. Political connections can also play a significant role, as investors navigate zoning laws and regulations to secure approvals for their developments.

This chapter delves into the power of networks, illustrating how these billionaires leverage their connections to achieve their goals. By examining the role of relationships in their success, we gain insights into the importance of networking and collaboration in building empires.

CHAPTER 9: THE POWER OF NETWORKS

The power of networks highlights the value of fostering strong relationships and seeking mentorship and collaboration. It offers valuable lessons for aspiring entrepreneurs and investors looking to build their own networks and achieve success.

10

Chapter 10: Navigating Regulation and Policy

Regulation and policy can significantly impact the fortunes of both tech and real estate billionaires. Innovators must navigate complex regulatory landscapes, balancing innovation with compliance. Real estate investors face zoning laws, environmental regulations, and political factors that can affect their projects.

Tech innovators often encounter regulatory challenges related to data privacy, antitrust laws, and intellectual property. Companies like Apple and Microsoft have had to navigate legal battles and adapt to changing regulations to protect their interests and maintain market dominance. Their ability to balance innovation with compliance is crucial to their sustained success.

Real estate investors face a different set of regulatory challenges. Zoning laws and environmental regulations can impact the feasibility and profitability of their projects. Investors must engage with local governments, advocacy groups, and community stakeholders to secure approvals and ensure their developments align with regulatory requirements. This involves strategic planning, negotiation, and sometimes legal action.

This chapter explores the regulatory challenges faced by these groups and their strategies for influencing and adapting to policy changes. By examining their approaches to navigating regulation and policy, we gain insights into

CHAPTER 10: NAVIGATING REGULATION AND POLICY

the complexities of operating in highly regulated industries.

Understanding how Silicon Valley innovators and real estate investors navigate regulation and policy offers valuable lessons for those looking to thrive in their respective fields. It underscores the importance of strategic planning, compliance, and advocacy in achieving long-term success.

11

Chapter 11: The Future of Wealth

As we look to the future, the landscapes of Silicon Valley and real estate are poised for transformation. Emerging technologies, shifting economic dynamics, and evolving societal values will shape the next generation of billionaires. This chapter speculates on the future of wealth, considering the trends and innovations that will drive growth in both sectors.

The rise of artificial intelligence, blockchain, and other emerging technologies presents new opportunities for tech innovators. These advancements have the potential to revolutionize industries, create new business models, and generate immense wealth. Innovators who can harness these technologies and adapt to changing market conditions will continue to drive progress and shape the future.

Real estate investors will also need to adapt to changing market dynamics and societal values. The growing emphasis on sustainability, smart cities, and affordable housing will influence investment strategies and project development. Investors who prioritize sustainability and social responsibility will be well-positioned to capitalize on these trends and contribute to the growth of resilient, inclusive communities.

This chapter explores the forces that will define the future of these empires, offering insights into the opportunities and challenges that lie ahead. By examining the emerging trends in Silicon Valley and real estate, we gain a

CHAPTER 11: THE FUTURE OF WEALTH

deeper understanding of the future landscape of wealth.

The future of wealth underscores the importance of adaptability, innovation, and social responsibility. It offers valuable lessons for aspiring entrepreneurs and investors looking to navigate the evolving landscape and achieve success.

12

Chapter 12: Lessons from the Titans

The journeys of Silicon Valley and real estate billionaires offer valuable lessons for aspiring entrepreneurs and investors. This chapter distills the key insights from their experiences, highlighting the principles and strategies that have propelled them to the pinnacle of success. Whether you're an innovator dreaming of the next big tech breakthrough or an investor eyeing lucrative real estate opportunities, these lessons provide a roadmap for achieving your own ambitions.

One key lesson is the importance of embracing failure and learning from it. Both tech innovators and real estate investors understand that setbacks are an inevitable part of the journey. By viewing failures as opportunities for growth and improvement, they develop resilience and the ability to persevere through challenges.

Another lesson is the value of strategic thinking and long-term vision. Successful billionaires are able to identify and seize opportunities while maintaining a focus on their overarching goals. They balance risk and reward, leveraging their expertise and networks to make informed decisions that drive their success.

This chapter also emphasizes the importance of innovation, adaptability, and social responsibility. By embracing new technologies, adapting to changing market conditions, and prioritizing the well-being of their communities, these billionaires are able to create lasting impact and achieve sustained success.

By drawing lessons from the experiences of Silicon Valley and real estate billionaires, aspiring entrepreneurs and investors can gain valuable insights and strategies for achieving their own ambitions. It offers a roadmap for navigating the complex landscape of wealth-building and creating a lasting legacy.

Innovators vs. Investors: A Human Comparison of Silicon Valley and Real Estate Billionaires

In this captivating exploration of wealth and success, "Innovators vs. Investors: A Human Comparison of Silicon Valley and Real Estate Billionaires" delves into the fascinating worlds of two distinct types of billionaires. Through twelve engaging chapters, the book compares and contrasts the lives, mindsets, and journeys of tech innovators and real estate moguls.

From the dawn of their empires to the impact they have on society, the book examines the origins, mindsets, and educational backgrounds that shape these titans of industry. Readers will gain insights into the risk and reward profiles that define their strategies, as well as their approaches to navigating economic challenges and regulatory landscapes.

The book also highlights the philanthropic endeavors of these billionaires, showcasing their contributions to society and the motivations behind their giving. By exploring the influence of technology and the power of networks, readers will understand the innovative approaches that drive their success.

As we look to the future, the book speculates on the emerging trends and innovations that will shape the next generation of billionaires. With valuable lessons from the journeys of Silicon Valley and real estate leaders, "Innovators vs. Investors" offers a roadmap for aspiring entrepreneurs and investors seeking to achieve their own ambitions.

Through detailed case studies, thought-provoking analysis, and compelling narratives, this book provides a comprehensive and humanized comparison of two worlds that continue to shape our economy and society. Whether you're an aspiring entrepreneur, an investor, or simply curious about the dynamics of wealth, "Innovators vs. Investors" is an enlightening and inspiring read.

www.ingramcontent.com/pod-product-compliance
Lightning Source LLC
LaVergne TN
LVHW021055100526
838202LV00083B/6208